Images of Christmas

Solo Piano Arrangements

by

Lloyd Larson

CONTENTS

FOREWORD

What images come to mind when someone asks you to recall favorite Christmas memories? I suspect most of us remember experiences around the tree with our family. Perhaps they were experiences we had as children with extended family--grandparents, cousins, aunts and uncles. For some it may be that first Christmas we shared with our spouse or the initial one we experienced after our first child was born. Christmas memories also usually include food! Traditional holiday favorites which may be unique to our own personal or family traditions . . . those specially designed holiday cookies or the annual Christmas dinner with all the fixings that only Grandma knows how to do just right!

For me one of the images which comes to mind is hot weather, lakes and a swimming pool! I know that seems a little odd, but you see I am from a large family living in various states throughout the midwest. As a result, we annually gather in Arkansas in early July to vacation together. While we are together, we also celebrate our family Christmas . . . "Christmas in July" as we call it!

Living in Minnesota, I also have panoramic images in my mind of snow-laden yards, fields and forests making almost the darkest night seem bright as day! I can feel the brisk wintry wind on my face as I enjoy a walk on a frozen lake and marvel at the magnanimous display of stars in God's heaven. The smell of burning fireplaces, the crisp sound of ringing bells, and the dazzling array of Christmas lights throughout our neighborhood and community cause me to marvel anew at the sense of hope and wonder which is stirred in each of us at Christmas.

Some of the most vivid images which come to my mind are related to meaningful worship experiences; gathering in my home church with other believers to celebrate the birth of Jesus. Perhaps for others it may include an Advent "Hanging of the Greens" service or the annual Christmas musical or pageant. Others, no doubt, recall a quietly meaningful candlelight or communion Christmas Eve service.

All of these images, though, are incomplete in my mind without adding the sounds of Christmas carols. In a day and age when the world around us is changing at the speed of light, there is something remarkably comforting and renewing about the familiar sounds of Christmas carols. It is inconceivable to imagine the holiday season without these melodies and words which have been deeply ingrained on our hearts over a life-time.

Though these carols are familiar and, in many cases, hundreds of years old, they come to us fresh and new each Advent and Christmas . . . just as the familiar story of our Savior's birth comes to us in new and fresh ways. It is my hope that these new piano settings of some of my favorite carols will enable you to refresh your own spirit and the spirits of those who will hear you play them. Though wrapped in new "packaging," they are the same wonderful carols which conjure up in each of us delightful and personal ***"images of Christmas"*** and remind us again of the joyous message: "To you is born this day in the city of David a Savior, who is Christ the Lord." Merry Christmas!

Lloyd Larson

Christmas Bells

Traditional Bell Carols
arranged by Lloyd Larson (ASCAP)

Lightly in "1" (𝅗𝅥 = ca. 69)
"Carol of the Bells" (Ukrainian Bell Carol)

cresc. poco a poco
f
dim. poco a poco

mf
dim. e rit.
Gently, freely (♩= ca. 80)
"I Heard the Bells on Christmas Day" (Jean Baptiste Calkin)
mp
dim.
molto rit.
p
rit.
mp
a tempo

accel. poco a poco
mf
f
rit.
With energy (♩= ca. 108)
"Ding Dong! Merrily on High" (16th C. French mel.)
a tempo

molto rit.
"Carol of the Bells" (Reprise)
= 69
ff
dim. poco a poco
f
mf
mp
dim. e rit.
p
f freely
8va

What Child Is This?

GREENSLEEVES (Traditional English mel., 16th C.)
arranged by Lloyd Larson (ASCAP)

cresc.
mf
dim. e rit.
p
a tempo
mp

mf
f

ff
dim. e rit.
mp a tempo
f
dim. e rit.
mp freely, slowly

Angel Carols

Traditional Carols
arranged by Lloyd Larson (ASCAP)

dim. e rit.

(♩= ca. 108)
"Angels from the Realms of Glory" (Henry T. Smart)
mp
pedal lightly
mf
f
"Angels We Have Heard on High" (18th C. French mel.)
mp
no pedal (thru M. 59)

mf
f
ff
Broadening to end
molto rit.
fff
8vb

Coventry Carol

Traditional English mel., 16th C.
***arranged by* Lloyd Larson (ASCAP)**

mp
mf
p
mp

mf
p
mp
rit.
mp a tempo
cresc. poco a poco
mf
f

ff
dim. e rit.
mf
mp
freely, slowing
dim.
pp

On This Day Earth Shall Ring

PERSONENT HODIE *(Piae Cantiones)*
arranged by Lloyd Larson (ASCAP)

dim.

mp
mf
f

mf
molto rit.
freely
8va
Ped.

In the Bleak Midwinter

CRANHAM (Gustav Holst)
arranged by Lloyd Larson (ASCAP)

Passionately, freely throughout (♩ = ca. 76)

mp
mf
f
dim. e rit.
mp freely
dim. e rit.
pp

God Rest Ye Merry, Gentlemen

Traditional English Carol
arranged by Lloyd Larson (ASCAP)

mp
mf

f
ff

f
ff
mf
molto rit.

Sing We Now of Christmas

NOEL NOUVELET (Traditional French Carol)
arranged by Lloyd Larson (ASCAP)

8va
pp
mf
dim. e rit.
Slowly, freely (♩= ca. 88)
mp
holding back
moving ahead
cresc. e accel. poco a poco
mf

f
ff
12
rit.
ten.
Tempo primo (♩= ca. 112)
mf
f
mf
f
mf
mp

mf
f
ff
rit.
15ma
black note gliss.
molto rit.

Once in Royal David's City

IRBY (Henry J. Gauntlett)
arranged by Lloyd Larson (ASCAP)

mf
mp

mf
f

ff
dim.
mf
molto rit.

While by the Sheep We Watched

JUNGST (Traditional German mel.)
arranged by Lloyd Larson (ASCAP)

Lightly, with movement (♩ = ca. 100)

p
mf
p
mp
f
mp

f
mp
f
mp
f
ff
rit.